Waiting in Joyful Hope

Daily Reflections for
Advent and Christmas 2008–2009

Bishop Robert F. Morneau

LITURGICAL PRESS
Collegeville, Minnesota

www.litpress.org

Nihil Obstat: Rev. Robert C. Harren, J.C.L., *Censor deputatus*.

Imprimatur: ✜ Most Rev. John F. Kinney, J.C.D., D.D., Bishop of St. Cloud, Minnesota, November 16, 2007.

In addition to the optional feasts of SS. Nicholas, Stephen, Thomas Becket, and John Neumann, there are other optional feasts not noted.

Shakespearean excerpts taken from *The Complete Works of Shakespeare*, ed. David Bevington, 3rd ed. (Genview, IL: Scott, Foresman and Company, 1980).

Cover design by Ann Blattner.

ISSN 1550-803X
ISBN: 978-0-8146-3081-5

Introduction

For the next six weeks, millions of Christians from around the globe will be pondering the same Scripture passages, reflecting on the same mysteries of our faith, and striving to experience the same promise of peace that lies at the heart of our Advent and Christmas liturgies. As a community and as individuals we will experience once again the invitation to participate in the very life of God as offered to us through the person of Jesus. And, as members of a diverse global community, we will be challenged to promote the peace and justice that is at the heart of the kingdom of God.

As we strive to grow spiritually we do have to contend with a variety of forces that distract us from our union with God and our unity with one another. Consumerism has the effect of filling our lives with material things, leaving little room for divine things. Excessive busyness puts us in a hurried mode, making loving attention, that is, contemplation, very difficult. Add to this list the struggle to make a daily living, the conflicts in our personal relationships, and that ever-present disease of narcissism and we know that Advent will demand intense effort and more than a modicum of grace.

But that grace is there. God continually seeks us out in the messiness of life. God's light, love, and life are available every hour of every day. We need but turn within for divine assistance; we need but look about us to the glory of God in the stars, in the compassion of those who serve the poor, in the prophets calling us to justice.

Although all of us have our unique vocation, we each are called to nurture that mutual dialogue with God that we call prayer. This intimate communication between Creator and creature is wonderfully mysterious and yet wonderfully simple. It's about listening and responding. God speaks the divine word of love and mercy; we respond in gratitude and praise. We speak to our God about whatever is going on in our lives . . . and God responds with that compassion and peace that is beyond all understanding.

In these daily reflections for the Advent and Christmas seasons, the Lectionary is the starting point for prayer. The Scripture references for each day are given along with a short passage from one of the readings. Then a reflection is offered to stimulate our thinking about God's word. This is followed by some meditative questions and a short prayer. The process used is an adaptation of *lectio divina*. This "sacred reading" is the starting point. It is followed by *meditatio* (meditating on the word), *oratio* (tasting the word in our heart), and *contemplatio* (resting in the silence of God's presence).

Perhaps Advent is all about the advice given at a wedding homily. The celebrant told the couple about to be married that if they wanted to have a happy marriage (we might add a happy life or a happy Advent/Christmas season), they should do four things: "Live simply, serve generously, care deeply, speak kindly." God's word calls us to simplicity, generosity, compassion, and kindness. God's word invites us into the very life of Jesus. By pondering God's word and putting it into practice, we become authentic disciples and agents of God's peace and justice.

FIRST WEEK OF ADVENT

Grace: Friendship with God

Readings: Isa 63:16b-17, 19b; 64:2-7; 1 Cor 1:3-9; Mark 13:33-37

Scripture:
God is faithful,
and by him you were called to fellowship with his Son,
Jesus Christ our Lord. (1 Cor 1:9)

Reflection: Advent, like all liturgical seasons, is about deepening our relationship with God. That relationship is one of friendship. We are invited into an intimate, mutual, loving fellowship with the Lord.

Our Advent disposition is one of attentiveness. The gospel passage from Mark has a sense of urgency in that we are called to be watchful, to stay awake, to be on guard. Jesus, our brother and friend, is constantly breaking into our lives through sacraments and Scripture, through our encounter with others and in the inner movements of our heart. By responding in obedience to the Lord's advances, we deepen our friendship with our Lord. And it is by living gospel values that we come to know the Lord Jesus, not abstractly, but with a knowledge that is experiential and enduring. Our call is to be God-like, putting on the mind and heart of Jesus. We are to put into action the Christian values of love, forgiveness, and compassion.

Isaiah's relationship with God is characterized by intimacy and mutuality, two essential qualities of friendship. The prophet even chides God for letting us wander. He accuses God of hiding his face from us. But, in the end, Isaiah settles down and admits that God is the potter and we are the work of the divine hand. Any type of wandering or hardness of heart comes, not from God, but from our misuse of freedom. Sin weakens, can even destroy, our friendship with God.

Friendship is characterized by giving. Saint Paul reminds the Corinthians that they have been richly endowed. They have been given not only the gifts of knowledge and speech but the very gift of God himself: uncreated grace. Such is the fidelity of the Divine Giver, of our Divine Friend.

Advent is about friendship; it's all about how faithful God is in his love for us in Jesus. During Advent, we respond to God's initiative and by so doing come to know that peace and joy that are beyond all understanding.

Meditation: Why did St. Thomas Aquinas describe grace as *amacitia Dei*—friendship with God? During Advent we can deepen that friendship through prayer, by recognizing Christ in others, and by being responsive to what God asks of us.

Prayer: Faithful God, we tend to wander from your constant friendship. Continue to gift us with watchful hearts so that as you come into our daily lives, we might be open to your love and come to witness that love in our concern for others. Help us to be aware of your kindness; in your mercy, grant us your salvation. Come, Lord Jesus, come.

Inclusivity: God's Plan

Readings: Isa 2:1-5; Matt 8:5-11

Scripture:
I say to you, many will come from the east and the west,
and will recline with Abraham, Isaac, and Jacob
at the banquet in the Kingdom of heaven. (Matt 8:11)

Reflection: Pope John XXIII once shared the secret of his ministry: a crucifix hanging in his bedroom. It reminded the Pope, upon retiring at night or getting up in the morning, that the open arms of the crucified Jesus was a symbol of the Lord's inclusive love and mercy. John XXIII commented: "No one is excluded from his love, from his forgiveness." Those who witnessed the short term of John XXIII's papacy realized that he lived out that conviction.

We witness the inclusivity of that love in today's gospel as Jesus heals the centurion's serving boy. Impressed with the centurion's faith, Jesus goes on to share a vision of the eternal banquet to which many who are not officially "believers" will come. This sense of the universality of salvation is something we need to ponder during this Advent season. For is it not true that many individuals who are not institutional Christians are building the kingdom by being agents of truth and charity, freedom and justice?

Isaiah's vision in our first reading reflects a similar inclusivity. The prophet speaks of the days to come when all nations will stream to the mountain of the Lord. This vision is one of peace wherein swords and spears will be transformed into pruning hooks and plowshares. Whether on the mountain or under the cross, God gives us a divine instruction: love, forgive, be compassionate to all. When we fulfill that instruction, we are walking in the light of the Lord and we experience joy and peace.

Jesus' inclusivity and Isaiah's vision are thwarted by racism. Because people are of different ethnic backgrounds they are often discriminated against, denied rights to an education, employment, housing, and other needs. Exclusion happens also because of gender and other differences among peoples. The unity and oneness that Jesus desired is fragmented. The peace of God's kingdom is not experienced.

As Advent people we are to embrace others with open arms; we are to walk in the light of the Lord and share with others God's compassion. Then, perhaps, Jesus will be amazed at the depth of our faith and love.

Meditation: How inclusive are you in dealing with people different from yourself? Pray for the gift of hospitality during this season of Advent.

Prayer: Compassionate Jesus, continue to heal our broken world. Though we know that we are not worthy to come under your roof, may our faith in your love draw us ever closer to your mountain of peace. May the weapons of destruction be transformed into technology for peace. May all who suffer from any illness feel the touch of your gentle compassion.

December 2: Tuesday of the First Week of Advent

The Gift of Revelation

Readings: Isa 11:1-10; Luke 10:21-24

Scripture:
For I say to you,
> many prophets and kings desired to see what you see,
> but did not see it,
> and to hear what you hear, but did not hear it.
> (Luke 10:24)

Reflection: Jonathan Edwards (1703–1758), a noted Puritan theologian, is famous for his 1741 sermon "Sinners in the Hand of an Angry God." Unfortunately, he has been identified solely with this preaching whereas his theology is much richer because the God he came to know and love was a God of beauty, mercy, and love. What Edwards saw and what he heard was grounded in a conversion experience that forever changed his life. The experience of God's love in Jesus gave Edwards a new vision and a whole new way of life.

We all struggle with dullness of mind and weakness of will. We need the gifts of God if we are to see God's glory and hear God's truth. Isaiah the prophet speaks of those transforming gifts: wisdom, understanding, counsel, strength, knowledge, and fear of the Lord. It is only when these graces are offered and received that we will, individually and as a community, be able to act as agents of justice and peace.

Luke's gospel reminds us that Jesus rejoiced in the Holy Spirit and the Spirit's work. It was through the Spirit's ministry of revelation that children, not the learned and clever, came to an awareness of God's creative, redeeming love. The disciples too, because they walked with the Lord, were given eyes of faith and saw salvation history in action. The Holy Spirit gave them a new vision and a whole new way of life.

John Ruskin wrote: "The greatest thing a human soul ever does in this world is to see something. . . . To see is poetry, prophecy, and religion, all in one." Seeing is a difficult art, as is hearing. Too often we judge by appearance or hearsay, as Isaiah tells us. It is only when God's Spirit is upon us that we will truly see reality for what it is, that we will be able to hear the truth in all its purity.

Meditation: Why is seeing and hearing so difficult for us? Advent affords us a wonderful opportunity to practice the art of seeing and listening. Take notes on your observations and conversations and discern the presence or absence of the Lord in them.

Prayer: Come, Holy Spirit, send your gifts of wisdom and understanding upon us. Help us to see the beauty of your glory; help us to hear the message of your love and forgiveness. We pray that justice may flourish in our world; we pray that the fullness of peace will be ours. May this Advent be a time of revelation and a time of courageous commitment to your kingdom.

December 3: Memorial of St. Francis Xavier, Priest
(Catholic Church)

Wednesday of the First Week of Advent
(Episcopal Church)

The Eucharistic Mountain

Readings: Isa 25:6-10a; Matt 15:29-37

Scripture:
Then he [Jesus] took the seven loaves and the fish,
    gave thanks, broke the loaves,
        and gave them to the disciples, who in turn gave them to
        the crowds.
They all ate and were satisfied. (Matt 15:36-37a)

Reflection: Belden Lane, a professor at St. Louis University, wrote an important work on the role of story and place in spirituality. His volume, *Landscapes of the Sacred: Geography and Narrative in American Spirituality*, traces the spiritual traditions of Native Americans, early French and Spanish communities, the Puritans and Shakers, as well as the Catholic Worker movement. Each of these spiritualities was grounded in sacred space; each of these traditions had a story to relate.

The Scriptures, be they the writings of Isaiah or one of the gospels, is about place and story. In today's readings the mountain is a symbol of God encountering humankind. This geography bridges heaven and earth; the mountain is the site of transformation and grace.

Jesus leaves the sea (another sacred geography) and goes up the mountain. A number of things happen there: healing, teaching, feeding. Jesus is presented as an agent of life, as an agent of the Father's rich compassion. Aware of the suffering of the ill, and sensitive to the hunger of the crowds, Jesus responds. The blind and lame are cured; the hungry are fed and leave satisfied.

Isaiah also describes mountainous events. On God's mountain a feast is held, and besides providing fine food and wines, God wipes away the tears of suffering and even death itself. Sins are forgiven and salvation is bestowed upon those who make the journey into God's presence. And the people's response? They rejoice and are glad at the marvelous deeds of the Lord.

If the mountain is a symbol of sacred geography, the Eucharist is a sign of the sacred story. It's a story of God's love expressed in feeding the hungry and healing the ill. It's a story of forgiveness and compassion. It's a story of divine mercy and the promise of justice. It's the original love story.

Meditation: What are the sacred spaces in your life and what story can be told in that setting? Spend some time seeing in your mind's eye the most important place in your life. Return to it and ask God to reveal how grace was offered to you there.

Prayer: Lord Jesus, draw us up to your mountain. May we experience there the mystery of your love and the healing power of your hand. We need your compassion; we need to taste again the food of life, the Eucharist.

December 4: Thursday of the First Week of Advent
St. John of Damascus, Priest and Doctor of the Church

God's Will

Readings: Isa 26:1-6; Matt 7:21, 24-27

Scripture:
Jesus said to his disciples:
"Not everyone who says to me, 'Lord, Lord,'
    will enter the Kingdom of heaven,
    but only the one who does the will of my Father in
        heaven." (Matt 7:21)

Reflection: C. S. Lewis, an influential Anglican writer, maintained that there are but two types of people on this earth: those who do God's will and those who do their own. Many see in Lewis's Chronicles of Narnia series a struggling between what God is asking of the characters and the characters' own plans. This emphasizes for readers that only when our will is aligned with God's will is peace possible.

What is God's will? Micah the prophet gives us a nutshell version of the divine design: we are to act justly, we are to love tenderly, and we are to walk humbly with our God (Mic 6:8). Isaiah the prophet is in line with that vision in today's first reading. His vocabulary is slightly different but the message is the same. We do God's will by trusting in the Lord, by keeping faith, by singing the song of God's love and providence. Ultimately, God's will is our salvation, that we all may be one with God, and that we might then experience unity among ourselves. Where unity exists, joy and peace overflow as by-products of the love that leads to oneness.

Jesus speaks about two categories of people: the wise and the foolish. The analogy of building a house is fitting. For certain, the rain and wind will come with great force. The wise who build well will withstand the storms; the foolish, failing to see nature's harsh consequences, will experience disaster.

In our spiritual life we come to realize that words—"Lord, Lord"—are not enough. We must put Gospel values into action. A central part of discipleship is sharing in the suffering of Jesus. Wise Christians know that this is part of the baptismal promise and are not surprised or discouraged when crosses come; the foolish, romanticizing the Christian journey, attempt to exempt themselves from the harsh demands of the Gospel.

Advent wisdom is a powerful gift and we don't have to wait until Christmas to open it.

Meditation: Pray the "Our Father" with great devotion. What do you experience when you ask that God's kingdom might come, that God's will be done? Recount the times in your life when you experienced peace. Were these not the times when you were doing God's will?

Prayer: Spirit of wisdom, grant us the grace of discernment. May we come to know your will and may we have the courage to do it. Break our willfulness; cleanse us of fear. Then, we will joyfully set off on the royal road to your kingdom.

Confidence

Readings: Isa 29:17-24; Matt 9:27-31

Scripture:
Then he touched their eyes and said,
  "Let it be done for you according to your faith."
And their eyes were opened. (Matt 9:29-30a)

Reflection: "Three blind mice, three blind mice, see how they run . . ." This nursery rhyme has its origin in history. Queen Mary I, also known as "Bloody Mary," had three noblemen executed. This event was reflected, sadly, in what we might think of as a "cute" children's nursery rhyme. On both the Catholic and Protestant sides of Reformation history, leaders failed to see and respect the dignity of the human person.

Two blind men, two blind men! Here we have another historical event. But this time we see the darkness of tragedy transformed by Jesus' healing touch, Jesus who is the light of the world. Two things should be noted: Jesus' compassion for the blind men and the deep confidence and faith these men had in Jesus. It is precisely at the intersection of divine mercy and human faith that salvation happens.

Isaiah the prophet extends the range of God's providential love in his vision of a world in which the deaf hear, the poor find joy, and the tyrant and arrogant are banished. And what is the cause of this salvific work? Obviously, the power of

God, but also the reverence and awe, that is, the faith and confidence, of the people who keep God's name holy.

In his gripping work *Into Thin Air: A Personal Account of the Mount Everest Disaster*, Jon Krakauer states that when climbing a mountain, the confidence that fellow climbers have in each other is of great importance. In the case of the two blind men in the gospel, the confidence of one or the other probably played a major role in their bold approach to Jesus. Again, the social nature of our spirituality cannot be stressed enough.

Advent is a season of faith, trust, and confidence. May we be given the grace to truly believe that the Lord, who is our light and our salvation, is near. Here! Now!

Meditation: What is your level of confidence and faith in the providence of God? Review how the Lord, over the years, has granted you sight. Practice looking with great awareness into the eyes of those you meet this day.

Prayer: Lord, we desire to see the truth and we yearn for the gift of your love. Deepen our faith in your power to transform us and the world. May we be confident that the poor will find peace, the lowly will find joy, the deaf will hear. For, as you know Lord, we are the poor, the lowly, and the deaf. We truly believe that you will heal us and restore all creation to your Father. Help us to see your providential love in all the events of our lives.

Spiritual Gerunds

Readings: Isa 30:19-21, 23-26; Matt 9:35–10:1, 5a, 6-8

Scripture:
Jesus went around to all the towns and villages,
   teaching in their synagogues,
   proclaiming the Gospel of the Kingdom,
   and curing every disease and illness. (Matt 9:35)

Reflection: Gerunds are verbal nouns. They are formed by taking verbs, for example, teach or proclaim, and adding "ing" to them: teaching/proclaiming. There are four gerunds in today's gospel that we are invited to participate in.

Teaching. A central ministry in the life of Jesus was that of communicating the truth. In various synagogues, on various mountainsides, Jesus taught about the mysteries of creation, redemption, and sanctification. We are the recipients of that body of knowledge. Our task is to learn it well, live it deeply, and teach it to those entrusted to our care.

Proclaiming. "Go, Tell It on the Mountain" is a song of proclamation. The message here is that God is near, close at hand. The kingdom is not some distant reality but is happening in the present moment. As agents of the kingdom, we proclaim in deed and word that God's love and mercy is for all.

Curing. Jesus is the Lord of compassion. In seeing the ill and hurting, Jesus is stirred with pity and reaches out to them. So many people are troubled; so many are abandoned. Jesus longs for his ministry of reconciliation to be continued by more and more laborers being sent into the harvest.

Instructing. Though similar to teaching, instructions have more to do with imperatives, that is, commands to do things. In this gospel passage the twelve disciples are told to go and seek out the lost sheep of the house of Israel.

Saint Nicholas, a fourth-century bishop, lived these spiritual gerunds. He taught and proclaimed, he cured and instructed. He is especially noted for his generosity and thus he fulfilled another instruction of Jesus. The gifts we have received without cost are to be given to others without cost. It is no surprise that this good stewardship is an expression of discipleship.

Meditation: What is the unique call you are being asked to respond to this Advent? Note carefully any special gift that you have received recently. How are you sharing that gift with others?

Prayer: Lord Jesus, through baptism you invite us to participate in the fullness of your life. Help us to teach well those you have entrusted to us; help us to proclaim in word and deed the good news that the kingdom has come; help us to heal and cure the hurts of our world. May we, like St. Nicholas, be generous, caring disciples.

SECOND WEEK OF ADVENT

December 7: Second Sunday of Advent

Our Concept of God

Readings: Isa 40:1-5, 9-11; 2 Pet 3:8-14; Mark 1:1-8

Scripture:
Like a shepherd he feeds his flock;
  in his arms he gathers the lambs,
carrying them in his bosom,
  and leading the ewes with care. (Isa 40:11)

Reflection: Our concept of God is at the heart of spirituality. If our idea of God is distorted, undeveloped, or erroneous, every other dimension of our spiritual journey will be adversely affected. During Advent, as we approach the Christmas mystery, we do well to reflect upon who God is for us and how our concept of God has evolved over time.

The prophet Isaiah gives us a powerful image of God: a caring, good shepherd. This shepherd, according to Isaiah, does four things: feeds, gathers, carries, and leads. God not only created us, but sustains, that is, feeds us. All life comes from God. We tend to scatter, even get lost, time and time again. Our Good Shepherd gathers us together in community, longing for all to be one. Often we grow weary and suffer disappointment. Though we may not realize it, God carries us during these times. With God's guidance, we are led into deeper commitment and more joyful service. Isaiah's God is caring, compassionate, and challenging.

Saint Peter's letter gives us some information about the nature of God. God is a promise maker and a promise keeper. God shows generous patience in dealing with his creatures. The divine plan is that none be lost, but all come to repentance. God's justice will bring about a new heaven and a new earth. God is on the move.

And what does the passage from Mark's gospel have to say about God? God sends messengers. Mary experienced that fact in the annunciation from the angel Gabriel. King David received God's message through the prophet Nathan. John the Baptist, while in the womb, stirred for joy when God himself, incarnate within Mary, came to him and his mother Elizabeth. God is constantly instructing us in his ways.

By praying the Scriptures with reverence, we come to know that God is a loving, caring, forgiving, compassionate God.

Meditation: Who is God for you? Take some time during Advent to chart how your knowledge of God has grown. List the people, the books, the events that shape your understanding of the nature of God.

Prayer: O Holy Trinity, send your Spirit into our minds and hearts. Help us to understand who you are; help us to love you freely and faithfully. Our minds are so limited; our hearts, so narrow. Come, Holy Spirit, for without your assistance we will live in ignorance and fear.

December 8: The Solemnity of the Immaculate Conception
(Catholic Church)

Monday of the Second Week of Advent
(Episcopal Church)

Fiat—Ave; Deo Gratias

Readings: Gen 3:9-15, 20; Eph 1:3-6, 11-12; Luke 1:26-38

Scripture:
And coming to her, he said,
"Hail, full of grace! The Lord is with you." (Luke 1:28)

Reflection: The claim is made that Latin is a dead language. Yet, crossword puzzles in our daily newspaper have participants figuring out *Carpe diem*, or *Cogito ergo sum*, or *Anno Domini*. Perhaps Latin is not as dead as we thought.

One Latin word—*Ave*—bears reflection. The full text is *Ave Maria, gratia plena* ("Hail Mary, full of grace"). One commentator maintained that to be full of grace is to have knowledge of being loved. Mary was chosen; Mary was loved; Mary was full of grace. What an awesome responsibility it was for the angel Gabriel to be given such an assignment. Yet, all of us have been loved by God, and angels have been sent our way to convince us that we too are chosen and loved by God. The messengers of this good news have sometimes been our parents or siblings, friends and even strangers. We do well during this Advent season to listen for the *Aves* that are addressed to us.

On this glorious feast of Mary we are called to ponder Mary's *fiat*—her obedience in saying let it be done according to God's will. Though Mary was afraid and did not know what was happening when the angel came to her, she turned her life over to the Lord and was willing to obey God's will, whatever the cost. Thus, Mary is the model of obedience for all of us who profess our discipleship in the Lord Jesus. Her surrender in the face of obstacles demonstrates both the power of God's grace and how Mary cooperated with that grace.

The Latin expression *Deo gratias* is still remembered by the elders of the church. It was their response when, at the end of Mass, the priest would say: *Ite, missa est* ("Go, the Mass is ended"). The "thanks be to God" response was an expression of gratitude for the sacrament of the Eucharist and the celebration of our creation and redemption in the Lord Jesus.

Is Latin a dead language? Perhaps few still know it but the messages expressed above are still living and transforming lives.

Meditation: What role does Mary play in your spirituality? Do you sense that you too have been chosen and loved by God? By the end of this day, by word or example, try to communicate to someone you meet how precious they are.

Prayer: Mary, full of grace, intercede for us. Our journey is long and difficult. So many fears crowd in upon our hearts, and our minds often lack the knowledge of God's plan. Help us to be obedient like you; help us to come to know that we too are offered the grace of the Holy Spirit.

Decision Making

Readings: Isa 40:1-11; Matt 18:12-14

Scripture:
What is your opinion?
If a man has a hundred sheep and one of them goes astray,
    will he not leave the ninety-nine in the hills
    and go in search of the stray? (Matt 18:12)

Reflection: People who are highly pragmatic would probably suggest to the shepherd that he forget about the stray sheep and cut his losses. Better to have ninety-nine safe and sound than take a chance of leaving them unprotected for wolves to come and scatter, perhaps even kill, them.

But our God is too compassionate to be pragmatic. Every sheep is important and, so it seems, the more vulnerable a creature is the more attention it should be given. In the current articulation of Catholic social teaching we call this attitude "preferential option for the poor and vulnerable." It is one of seven principles that should guide our decision making as disciples of the Lord.

The other six principles of Catholic social teaching are the dignity of the human person; the call to family, community, participation; rights and duties; the dignity of work and the worker; solidarity; and, the care of creation. A close reading of Isaiah and other books of the Bible will provide evidence that these values and guidelines are present throughout God's word.

In today's passage from Isaiah we hear about comforting God's people, making straight the way of the Lord, witnessing how God carries lambs with care. Our God is a God who will risk everything lest anyone be lost. Yes, our God will risk even his Son for the salvation of the world.

It's a good thing that shepherds do not have councils. Surely, the advisors would suggest that the shepherd not go after the stray if doing so might endanger the flock. But God's thoughts are not ours; God's ways are different from conventional wisdom.

And the point of the story: we have all wandered and gone astray. So Jesus has come to bring us back home. And he will pay any price, even his life.

Meditation: What is your understanding of the principle: fundamental option for the poor? During this Advent season, reach out to a poor family or person in your area. Seek them out as the shepherd seeks out the lost.

Prayer: God of infinite compassion, we have all wandered in one way or another from your light and love. Continue to seek us out; help us, in turn, to reach out to others who are wandering and living in darkness and the shadow of death. Send your Spirit into our hearts so that the decisions we make will be in accord with your will.

Eagles' Wings

Readings: Isa 40:25-31; Matt 11:28-30

Scripture:
They that hope in the Lᴏʀᴅ will renew their strength,
    they will soar as with eagles' wings;
They will run and not grow weary,
    walk and not grow faint. (Isa 40:31)

Reflection: In his poem "The Windhover," the Jesuit poet Gerard Manley Hopkins brilliantly captures in words the soaring of an early morning hawk. So impressed was he by this feat that he cried out: "My heart in hiding / Stirred for a bird, – the achieve of, the mastery of the thing!"

Isaiah the prophet and poet was also in tune with nature. To describe people who have hope and who are strengthened by the Lord, Isaiah turned to the soaring of an eagle. Isaiah's heart in hiding was stirred; he marveled at the skill and mastery of an eagle's flight as it buffeted the wind.

It is God's strength and grace that empowers us to run the spiritual journey and not grow weary; it is God's constant providence that enables us to walk the path to Calvary with him and not grow faint. If we unite ourselves to Christ then our yoke will be easy to carry and what we considered a heavy, almost unbearable burden, will become light.

But to experience this hope and strength we must come to the Lord. Indeed, during this Advent time and every season of our life, Jesus invites us: "Come to me, all you who labor and are burdened, and I will give you rest" (Matt 11:28). This is an RSVP that we must answer in the affirmative lest life itself become too difficult to manage. Just as we need proper nutrition and rest for our physical well-being, so too do we need God's constant care to stay spiritually healthy.

The meek and the humble know their intrinsic poverty. No pretense here. We cannot claim autonomy when it comes to spiritual growth. We depend on God's strength for our survival as much as a fish depends on the water, birds on the air.

Meditation: In what lie your hope and your strength? Is there someone in your family or workplace who is carrying a heavy burden? What can you do to help lighten their cross? What can you do to allow others to help you with your cross?

Prayer: Lord God, our journey here on earth is long and often difficult. Often we grow weary, sometimes we get discouraged. Be with us and our fellow pilgrims as we strive to maintain our hope. May we soar like eagles, achieve the mastery of the windhover. And do all this for your glory.

December 11: Thursday of the Second Week of Advent

Comparisons

Readings: Isa 41:13-20; Matt 11:11-15

Scripture:
Amen, I say to you,
  among those born of women
  there has been none greater than John the Baptist.
    (Matt 11:11)

Reflection: There is a proverb that warns us: "Comparisons are odious." Just ask any twin, any child with a smarter or more talented older sibling, or any team that a coach compares to a previous championship team. Just because our language provides such words as "great, greater, greatest," or "good, better, best," does not mean that the words should necessarily be used. Comparisons can hurt.

Yet Jesus says that no person born of woman is greater than John the Baptist. For Jesus to make such a statement demands our attention. In what lies John's greatness or, if you will, his "greaterness"?

John was sent on mission to prepare the way of the Lord. This mission was great because of John's single-mindedness, his complete commitment to what God asked of him. John was great because of his courage in standing up to Herod even though that courage resulted in John's execution. John was great because he was loved by God and, even while in the womb, he stirred for joy. Single-mindedness, courage, being loved— all are causes for greatness.

In the reading from Isaiah we come across some rather disturbing comparisons. Jacob is compared to a worm; Israel to a maggot. Yet the message of the prophet is that God will help and rescue his people. Though sin has caused corruption (thus the worm and maggot analogies), God's providence and compassion far transcend the human condition. In the end, like John the Baptist, Israel will rejoice in the Lord.

For critics, comparison may be helpful. Comparing John of the Cross to the Little Flower might provide some insight and new understanding. Comparing Augustine's *Confessions* with other spiritual autobiographies might prove an enriching experience. But appreciating the uniqueness of every individual and honoring his or her particular gifts is the preferred way to go. God has gifted each of us in different ways. Comparing ourselves with others can simply drain our energy or even cause discouragement.

Meditation: Do you find comparisons odious? During Advent it might be helpful to read a book like Robert Ellsberg's *All Saints*, not to compare yourself with these individuals, but to be challenged to grow and to use your gifts to the fullest. Name one gift you would like to nurture this Advent.

Prayer: Compassionate God, guide us in your ways. Like John the Baptist, may we come to understand what role you have assigned to us on our journey. Give us insight and courage; give us joy to do whatever you ask. Help us to appreciate the unique gifts of every individual and to honor them.

December 12: Feast of Our Lady of Guadalupe
(Catholic Church)

Friday of the Second Week of Advent
(Episcopal Church)

The Indwelling Spirit

Readings: Zech 2:14-17; Luke 1:26-38

Scripture:
And the angel said to her in reply,
"The Holy Spirit will come upon you,
and the power of the Most High will overshadow you."
(Luke 1:35a)

Reflection: In one poem, Emily Dickinson says that every soul has a guest. In our Christian tradition we call this the indwelling of the Holy Spirit. God not only creates and redeems us, God abides in the innermost room of our soul.

Mary is reminded of this by the angel Gabriel. The Holy Spirit will overshadow her and give her the strength to do God's will, despite fear and unknowing. This mysterious indwelling of God within us can be felt in moments of deep joy, firm peace, and committed love. It is a Spirit that transforms both our souls and our bodies. It is a Spirit of life.

We pray in today's preface: "Through the power of the Holy Spirit, she became the virgin mother of your only Son, our Lord Jesus Christ, who is for ever the light of the world." This power of the Holy Spirit does three things: enlightens, enkindles, and empowers. The mind is given a vision of the truth; the heart receives the flame of God's love, and our words and deeds flow out of a new source. Mary's response to God's request came not just by her willing it but through the grace of the Holy Spirit.

The prophet Zechariah exhorts the people of Zion to sing and rejoice. The cause for their song and joy is the presence of the Lord. The prophet writes: ". . . and he will dwell among you, and you shall know that the LORD of hosts has sent me to you" (Zech 2:15). God dwells not only within us but also among us. Mary knew this as she journeyed to see Elizabeth, only to discover that the Spirit was also working in Elizabeth's life. The power of the Holy Spirit is given not only to an individual but also to the community.

Advent focuses on the coming of Jesus. But Advent also is a season of the working of the Holy Spirit. It is the Spirit that prepares Mary and Elizabeth to be open to the Lord's coming. That same Holy Spirit works in us through our prayer, our service, and our sharing with others. God takes the initiative and we are called to cooperate with the action of grace.

Meditation: How conscious are you that you are the temple of the Holy Spirit? When have you felt the Holy Spirit working in you and in your family and community?

Prayer: Spirit of Jesus and the Father, we long to make room in our minds and hearts for your coming. Transform us from within; grace us with your power to do good. Through Mary's intercession, may we offer you a warm welcome.

December 13: Memorial of St. Lucy, Virgin and Martyr
(Catholic Church)

Saturday of the Second Week of Advent
(Episcopal Church)

The Gift of Sight

Readings: Sir 48:1-4, 9-11; Matt 17:9a, 10-13

Scripture:
He said in reply, "Elijah will indeed come and restore all
    things;
  but I tell you that Elijah has already come,
  and they did not recognize him but did to him whatever
    they pleased." (Matt 17:11-12)

Reflection: Saint Lucy is the patroness of Sicily and of those
afflicted with eye diseases. It is fitting, therefore, that we
intercede through her for the gift of sight and recognition of
the Lord's presence in our midst. Just as the people of Jesus'
day failed to see John the Baptist as the Lord's prophet and
previously failed to understand the ministry of Elijah, we
are often blind to the working of God in our lives.

The seeing we speak of is both physical and spiritual.
Spiritual sight is to see with the eyes of faith. One challenge
for every Christian is to see and embrace the fact that the
Son of Man, our Lord Jesus, is a suffering Messiah. It is only
with faith that we can accept the mystery of the cross. It is
only with faith that we understand that John the Baptist did
not give up his life in vain.

Saint John of the Cross, a mystic and doctor of the church, speaks of how God looks at us. Insofar as we "look" in the same way, we conform ourselves to the likeness of God. Saint John writes: "When God looks, He loves and grants favors." Sometimes we stare or are critical, or hold others in contempt—whereas God looks with love and transforms what is seen.

As Advent progresses there is less and less daylight. The darkness inhibits our seeing. But we are journeying, in the dark, toward Jesus, the light of the world. He is the one who explains that his Father is a God of compassion. He is the one who enlightens us to understand who we are and what life is all about.

Elijah and John the Baptist were agents of God's life. Their role as prophets was to tell the truth. They offered people a vision of God's kingdom. They challenged anyone and everyone who lived contrary to God's plan. Their ministry, like St. Lucy's, was to mediate God's life, indeed, God's love.

Meditation: Who has helped you to see with the eyes of faith? What is your vision of God's will? List the books, plays, poems, songs that have broadened your vision of faith.

Prayer: Saint Lucy, you experienced Jesus as the light and love of your life. You saw clearly that God loved you and that you were to transmit that love to others. You did this by your martyrdom, your total self-giving. Pray that we see clearly what really matters.

THIRD WEEK OF ADVENT

Sent by God

Readings: Isa 61:1-2a, 10-11; 1 Thess 5:16-24; John 1:6-8, 19-28

Scripture:
A man named John was sent from God.
He came for testimony, to testify to the light,
 so that all might believe through him. (John 1:6-7)

Reflection: God is in the business of sending people here, there, and everywhere. God sent a man named Isaiah to the Israelite people; God sent a man named Paul to the Gentiles; God sent a woman named Mother Teresa to the poor people of India; God sent a woman named the Little Flower, St. Therese of Lisieux, to people all over the world. And, of course, God sent a man named John to testify to Jesus, the light of the world.

What was the mission of those sent? Isaiah's task was to deliver a message that would scatter the darkness of evil and sin. It was a message proclaiming liberty to those in bondage, vindication and justice for the persecuted and poor, good news of God's favor. The whole intent was to move people to faith. The hope was that, in hearing of God's love and mercy, these prophetic figures would come to believe in their own people and then be willing to share with them what they had received from God.

Paul's task was to testify to the person of Jesus and to show how, through the Lord's life, death, and resurrection, we are saved. Paul urges people to deepen their faith by ceaseless prayer, constant thanksgiving, and honor of all prophecies. Paul was also a realist and knew that people could stifle the work of the Holy Spirit, so the great apostle reminds us that God calls each of us to be trustworthy.

John the Baptist was clear about his identity. His role, important as it was, was subordinate to the mission and ministry of Jesus. The Baptist's job was to till the soil and prepare people's minds and hearts to accept the seeds of faith. John's radical conviction of God's redeeming love in Jesus was a treasure he could not keep to himself. It had to be shared, whatever the cost.

Meditation: In what ways does God send you forth to enrich the faith of others? A good Advent practice: read a chapter of the Bible every day to deepen your faith. Prayerfully reflect on how you will use this reading to enrich your life and the lives of others.

Prayer: Lord, deepen our faith in your love and providence. Help us to realize that through baptism and confirmation we are sent to further your kingdom of truth and charity, of freedom and justice. Send your Spirit upon us and always make us grateful. We ask this in Jesus' name.

December 15: Monday of the Third Week of Advent

Power and Authority

Readings: Num 24:2-7, 15-17a; Matt 21:23-27

Scripture:
By what authority are you doing these things?
And who gave you this authority? (Matt 21:23b)

Reflection: Jesus refused to answer the question about the source of his authority and power. But we know from other Scripture sources that Jesus' power came from his Father. And it was a power to do good, to communicate the truth, to spread beauty, to share love. Each of us has some degree of power, that is, the ability to bring about or to prevent change. Power can be negative when we make decisions characterized by manipulation or exploitation. There are forms of sin that are all too familiar: physically abusing others, treating people as rungs on a ladder in order to get ahead, dominating the lives of those weaker than us. Jesus never used power in this fashion. He authored (authority) only goodness.

Graced power appears in the form of helping others and working with others in making the world a better place. Good parents, good teachers, good coaches are individuals who are concerned with the growth and well-being of others. Cooperation takes energy and then orders that energy for the betterment of the community. The ministry of our church, the work of United Way or Salvation Army or the Society of St. Vincent de Paul, are forms of power that promote justice and peace.

Where does our energy come from? In the third Eucharistic prayer we pray: "All life, all holiness comes from you." God is the source of all energy but we are like transformers and can take that energy, that power, and direct it toward good or evil. Such is the incredible responsibility of power.

George Eliot, in her novel *Middlemarch*, wrote: "It was a principle of Mr. Bulstrode to gain as much power as possible, that he might use it for the glory of God." That was also the purpose of Jesus' power: he defended the poor and power-less, healed the sick, forgave sinners and befriended those without friends. He came to restore all creation back to the Father. In this saving work we see God glorified.

Meditation: What is your attitude toward power? Chart the ways in which you are using your energy (power) during this season of Advent. In what ways do you use power as Jesus did? How might you better use your power to serve those without power? How can you empower others?

Prayer: God of power and love, help us to be responsible for the time and energy you give us. Make us good stewards of all your gifts, especially the gift of our freedom. We know that all power comes from you. We pray that the Spirit will guide its use.

December 16: Tuesday of the Third Week of Advent

Jesus: The Buttonholer

Readings: Zeph 3:1-2, 9-13; Matt 21:28-32

Scripture:
Jesus said to the chief priests and the elders of the people: "What is your opinion?" (Matt 21:28a)

Reflection: Socrates was famous for buttonholing people and, through incisive questions, leading them to new knowledge. Jesus had the art of buttonholing down to a science. Time and time again he engaged individuals in conversation and helped them grow in wisdom and self-understanding. Jesus asked what people went out into the desert to see; he asked whether it was permissible to do good or evil; he asked about the greatest of the commandments; he asked about who his mother and brothers and sisters were, and who his neighbors were.

In today's gospel Jesus seeks the opinion of the chief priests and elders regarding obedience to a father's will. Already we hear in the wings "Thy will be done" from the Our Father. The case Jesus gives is a no-brainer. Obedience lies not in saying we will do something but in actually doing what is asked. Further, it is faith that underlies obedience.

Jesus' mission was universal. He came to reconcile all creation to the Father. That includes chief priests and elders, tax collectors and prostitutes, Pharisees and Samaritans. Everyone is being called by Jesus to repentance and faith. All are called to walk the path of holiness, the perfection of love. This is what the Father asks of all his daughters and sons.

John Henry Cardinal Newman stated: "Our only safety lies in obedience; our only comfort in keeping it in view." Obedience to God's will is the path to both freedom and peace. There is a paradox here: how can we be free by doing another's will? Is not obedience in direct opposition to our liberty? One can almost sense that Socrates is just around the corner.

Two comments. What God asks of us (Micah's famous call that we act justly, love tenderly, and walking humbly with God) is the truth. Not to be obedient is to live a lie and thus to become slaves to our own willfulness. Second, peace—living in right relationships—is grounded in faith, a deep conviction of God's redeeming love.

Reflection: Spend a few moments thinking about what is on God's agenda and what is on yours. In other words, what does God will and what do you will? Pray during this season of Advent for the type of obedience that characterized Mary's "yes" to the angel Gabriel. What will it cost you to put God's will ahead of your own desires?

Prayer: Jesus, draw us more deeply into the mystery of your Father's will. We ask for the grace of obedience. Through your gifts of wisdom and courage, we will come to the truth and live this day as faithful and obedient servants following your footsteps. Come, Lord Jesus, come.

The Family Tree

Readings: Gen 49:2, 8-10; Matt 1:1-17

Scripture:
. . . Jacob the father of Joseph, the husband of Mary.
Of her was born Jesus who is called the Christ. (Matt 1:16)

Reflection: Adoption involves a serious choice. An infant is chosen to become part of a new web of relationships. Here in the United States, couples are spending large sums of money to travel to China or Russia to find a child to join their family. Years from now, many of those infants, now grown, will pause on their journey and ask the question: from whence did I come? Who were my birth parents and what were they like? Why did they give me up and send me on this mission?

Adoptive children are not alone in asking, from whence did I come? We all have our family tree, our mysterious genealogy. Going back century after century, we realize that we are a composite of so many people, indeed, so many cultures and languages. Who were our ancestors fourteen generations ago? Where did they live? What good deeds or crimes did they commit? What have we inherited from them by way of looks and intelligence? What genes did we inherit for long life or for good or bad health?

Jesus, the Son of God, was born of Mary. Tradition has it that Mary's parents were Anne and Joachim. Scripture records that Jesus' ancestry is rooted back through Joseph to Abraham. On this family tree we find some noble characters: the loving Ruth, the courageous David, the faithful Joseph. But we must carefully note what is not listed in Matthew's family tree and what his audience would have known: Rahab was a prostitute, David committed adultery and murder, and Abraham had trouble at times telling the truth. In other words, Jesus was born into our wounded, frail, sinful family.

This gospel passage drives home the fact that our God embraces all of humanity. In Jesus, our whole history is taken on. Jesus anoints our virtues; Jesus forgives our sins. Through Jesus, God becomes our partner in life. But our God knows us and experiences us from the inside. In this there is much consolation, namely, God's incredible compassion and concern for us.

Meditation: Take time during this Advent season to ponder your ancestry. Who are some of the people who have revealed God's love and compassion to you? Who are the members of your family tree who have obscured or concealed God's goodness from you? What are you revealing or concealing to those on your family tree? Bring them all to prayer.

Prayer: Jesus, born of Mary, you understand our human journey: its joys and sorrows, its challenges and possibilities. Help us to be kind in our relating to others for we do not know what they have inherited. Grace us with wisdom to pass on to future generations your love and mercy.

The Stuff of Dreams

Readings: Jer 23:5-8; Matt 1:18-25

Scripture:
When Joseph awoke,
   he did as the angel of the Lord had commanded him
   and took his wife into his home. (Matt 1:24)

Reflection: Carl Jung wrote an autobiographical book entitled *Memories, Dreams, Reflections*. The work traces the development of his thought and the experiences that shaped his heart. Dreams played a significant role for Jung since he saw them as a channel for coming to know the unconscious part of his life and thus as a way to grow in self-knowledge.

Dreams often appear in the Scriptures as a means by which God reveals his plan of salvation. The Old Testament Joseph was known as the "dreamer." Dreams got him into trouble by arousing the ire of his brothers who then responded by selling him into slavery. But later his dreams helped him in Egypt to become an important administrator (see Gen 37–45). The New Testament Joseph was also influenced by his dreams. In today's gospel Joseph encounters God's messenger who delivers some rather specific instructions. Joseph is told to accept Mary as his wife and take her into his home.

Shakespeare's Prospero is right on target: "We are such stuff / As dreams are made of, and our little life / Is rounded with a sleep." Were we to have an autobiography of St. Joseph, the husband of Mary, surely the central chapter would record the great dream that shaped the rest of Joseph's life. That dream and his willingness to hear and obey the will of God in it was the graced stuff of his life.

The Talmud, too, provides wisdom about dreams: "A dream not understood is like a letter not opened." Perhaps some dreams in our lives arise out of indigestion, too much sauerkraut or pizza. However, many dreams may well be instruments through which God is communicating his plan for our well-being. Advent is a good season to take seriously all the inner movements of our lives. Through the gift of discernment from the Holy Spirit, we will be able to sort out holy dreams from nightmares, to learn what God's will is for us, as St. Joseph did.

Meditation: Spend some time jotting down your daydreams and your night dreams. Prayerfully consider if they are the sources of divine revelation or not. Watch especially for dreams that recur. They may have a significant role in your growth toward self-understanding.

Prayer: God of day and God of night, you never cease to communicate with us. Open our minds and hearts to our rich tradition, the depth of your Scriptures, the wisdom figures you send us and, yes, the dreams that float into our consciousness. Send your Spirit of discernment that we might understand your message from whatever source we receive it. We ask this through Jesus, your Son and our Lord.

Deaf Heaven?

Readings: Judg 13:2-7, 24-25a; Luke 1:5-25

Scripture:
But the angel said to him, "Do not be afraid, Zechariah,
   because your prayer has been heard." (Luke 1:13a)

Reflection: In Sonnet 29, Shakespeare laments his plight:
"When, in disgrace with fortune and men's eyes, / I all alone
beweep my outcast state / And trouble deaf heaven with
my bootless cries . . ." Were Zechariah a poet, he too might
have written this verse, since he and his wife Elizabeth
longed for a son. But in the end, heaven was not deaf, for
God heard Zechariah's plea and a son was given to him and
his wife.

A similar situation is recorded in the first reading from the
book of Judges. Manoah and his wife were unable to bear
children. We can surmise that they too troubled "deaf
heaven" for an answer to their desire. Like Zechariah, the
angel was on the move and brought good news to Manoah
that his wife was pregnant and would bear a son. Not only
were their prayers answered but their son Samson was
blessed by the Lord, and the Spirit stirred deep within him.

Advent is a season of serious prayer. We come before the
Lord with all of our questions, anxieties, and fears. Like both
Elizabeth and Manoah's wife, we long for the gift of life. We

want our lives to be fruitful with good deeds and the further-ing of God's kingdom. Our faith reminds us that heaven is not deaf, that God hears the cry of the poor, those who ask, knock, and seek, and those who long to do the divine will. The answer to our prayers may not be what we expect or come within our timeline, but in the end, God works his gracious will in our lives.

In *Hamlet*, Shakespeare's king exclaims: "My words fly up, my thoughts remain below: / Words without thoughts never to heaven go." During this season, we weave together our thoughts and words in prayer, as Zechariah did, trusting that God will continue to break through the barrenness to bring us life.

Meditation: In prayer, do you request that God's will or your own be done? Ponder what went on in the heart of Zechariah and Elizabeth as they grew older. Did they question the ef-fectiveness of their prayer before God blessed them with the birth of their son John? Do you ever question the effective-ness of your prayer? How do you answer those who ask you what good it does to pray?

Prayer: Gracious God, you do listen to all our words and all the movements of our hearts. Often we seek what is not, in the long run, beneficial to our salvation. Often we question whether you listen to our requests. Deepen our faith, stir our hope. We know, deep down, that heaven is not deaf and that your providence is always at work.

December 20: Saturday of the Third Week of Advent

Weariness: A Grace?

Readings: Isa 7:10-14; Luke 1:26-38

Scripture:
Then Isaiah said:
  Listen, O house of David!
Is it not enough for you to weary men,
  must you also weary my God? (Isa 7:13)

Reflection: It is not too difficult to develop the knack of wearying others. In fact, even small children have perfected this skill as they drive their siblings or their parents crazy with incessant whining. Adults also are not amateurs in this realm. Our complaining about taxes, government, religion, work, and whatever else can make for a very boring evening or lifetime. All too easily we can weary one another.

One description of weariness is to have our patience, tolerance, or pleasure exhausted. Exhausted is the operative word. Not only can we exhaust those around us—and ourselves as well—but the weariness can reach to the heavens and tempt God to grow tired of us. At least, this is the concern and question that the prophet Isaiah raises. "Enough already," he seems to cry out. Stop opposing God's plan for fullness of life and get on with living according to God's will.

Mary is our model. She did not weary our Lord even though she struggled with fear and the unknown. Her "yes" was firm and decisive. She did not ask for several years of discernment. She did not make the Lord wait until she went to a counselor for advice. She committed herself because she believed that God's design was the very meaning of her life. And it was: Jesus would be born of her and the world would be saved.

In his poem "The Pulley," the Anglican priest/poet George Herbert (1593–1633) describes how God has bestowed all kinds of gifts on us, gifts such as beauty and wisdom and honor and pleasure. But then God stopped, withholding from us the gift of rest. This will be God's "pulley" to draw us home. Herbert concludes his poem with: "Let him be rich and weary, that at least, / If goodness lead him not, yet weariness / May toss him to my breast."

So, perhaps for us, weariness can become a grace. We weary of created things in the end and come to know that only in God can we find peace and rest.

Meditation: What is your experience of weariness? List the people who weary you; the people whom you weary. In a paradoxical way, how can weariness be a grace?

Prayer: Bountiful God, you gift us with so many blessings. Yet we are restless and long for the infinite. No "thing" totally satisfies us. We always want more. May the weariness we feel be a call to turn to you; may our restlessness be interpreted as a holy longing. Grant this through Jesus, our brother and friend and Lord.

FOURTH WEEK OF ADVENT

December 21: Fourth Sunday of Advent

The Reign of God

Readings: 2 Sam 7:1-5, 8b-12, 14a, 16; Rom 16:25-27;
Luke 1:26-38

Scripture:
. . . and the Lord God will give him the throne of David
  his father,
and he will rule over the house of Jacob forever,
and of his kingdom there will be no end. (Luke 1:32b-33)

Reflection: When Mary said yes to God's request that she
be the mother of Jesus, the consequences of that answer were
extensive. Not only would her life and that of Joseph be
changed forever, but the mystery of Jesus and his mission
would change all of history.

At the core of that mission was ruling and reigning. The
angel proclaimed that Jesus would be given the throne of
David. But we know that Jesus' reign is not political. Rather,
the rule that Jesus came to establish was located in the human
heart. The kingdom of God will come without end when
hearts are governed by love, compassion, and forgiveness.

Saint Paul's life was governed by the rule and reign of
Jesus. This apostle to the Gentiles preached Christ Jesus, the
one who revealed the mystery of God's plan that had been
hidden for so many years. The mystery was God's inclusive
love and the desire that all people be saved. Paul stressed

that belief and obedience are the two necessary conditions for those who want to be disciples and who long to turn their lives over to God's rule.

In the first reading we hear a prophecy: David's house and kingdom will endure forever; his throne will stand firm forever. We know what happened to David. It would be David's descendant through whom the prophecy would be fulfilled. Jesus is the true king; it is his reign and rule that is to govern our minds and hearts.

Julian of Norwich, the fourteenth-century mystic, received a revelation in which she saw God's reign and the site of it was in the souls of individuals. It was there that God found a resting place and an honorable city. Advent is the season in which we are to open our minds and hearts to the reign of God.

Meditation: What are the forces, attitudes, and behaviors that reign in your heart, that govern your life? What does "Your kingdom come" mean for you? Discuss with a friend your understanding of God's rule in our lives.

Prayer: Lord Jesus, grant us wisdom and courage: the wisdom to understand more deeply your desire to govern our lives, the courage to do whatever you ask of us. Help us to realize that your throne is within our hearts and your kingdom is one of eternal peace, especially when we are troubled.

Presentations: Examples of Stewardship

Readings: 1 Sam 1:24-28; Luke 1:46-56

Scripture:
"Now I, in turn, give him to the LORD;
   as long as he lives, he shall be dedicated to the LORD."
She left Samuel there. (1 Sam 1:28)

Reflection: Hannah presented her son Samuel to the Lord in the temple. Mary presented her son Jesus to the Lord as well. By so doing, these two women were dedicating the lives of their sons to the work of the Lord. Further, this ritual gesture meant that both Hannah and Mary understood that all life came from God and belonged to God. These presentations expressed their belief in that fact.

The conventional wisdom of our culture maintains that our children, our property, our life itself, basically belong to us. We are, as it were, absolute owners. Thus we can do with our relationships and possessions what we deem fit.

Hannah and Mary had a different take on life. Everything is gift. All is grace. We are stewards of our time, of our children, and of ourselves. One day we will have to give an accounting of what we have done with the years, people, and things the Lord has entrusted to us. Thus we see the wisdom of Hannah and Mary: immediately they professed that all belongs to the Lord and because of that they dedicated their sons to God's will.

The Lord indeed did great things for Hannah and Mary. The Lord does great things for us. We are given life, a variety of talents, different opportunities and challenges that can enrich our lives. Our initial response should be one of gratitude; our deeper response should be one of generosity. What has been given is to be shared.

Advent is drawing to a close. We have but a few days to complete our preparations for the feast of the Nativity. What better way might we do this than by kneeling before God and turning over to God everything that we have and are. Besides, it all belongs to God. But by our presentation, we acknowledge our creaturehood and come to a deeper understanding of our responsibility to be good stewards.

Meditation: What lessons can you learn from the example of Hannah and Mary? What have you dedicated to the Lord thus far on your journey? Why is faith and trust so fundamental to our Christian way of life?

Prayer: God, source of all life, help us to understand that all is gift. Every breath we take, every day and year, all our friends and family—all come from you and to you must return. May we be good stewards of all that has been given to us and may we be generous in sharing all your gifts with others.

December 23: Tuesday of the Fourth Week of Advent

The Grace of Freedom

Readings: Mal 3:1-4, 23-24; Luke 1:57-66

Scripture:
Immediately his mouth was opened, his tongue freed,
  and he spoke blessing God. (Luke 1:64)

Reflection: Freedom is one of the most prized values in our culture. Anything that threatens our God-given freedom—be it overly restrictive laws, discrimination, or domination by political or religious authority—will be opposed, sometimes even with violence. Freedom is a treasure of great price.

We witness in God's word today the freedom that was given to Zechariah. Because of his doubt and unbelief, he was unable to speak. But as soon as he aligned his thought with God's plan, he could once again communicate and he did so by blessing and praising God. When Zechariah confirmed Elizabeth's "He will be called John," his mouth opened and his tongue was freed.

All of us have to struggle with aligning our will with God's will. Every time we fail to do this, our authentic freedom is diminished. Sin enslaves us at every level: physical, psychological, and spiritual. Jesus came to set us free from our sin and our addictions. It is a freedom laden with responsibility. The wider our freedom, the more responsibility we have for ourselves and others.

However, sometimes the issue is not freedom, but unfreedom. So what are those areas of unfreedom? Physically, we can be addicted to tobacco, alcohol, drugs, and other substances. Psychologically, sometimes fear or anxiety reduces our freedom and incarcerates us in depression or despair. Spiritually, we lose our freedom through sin, a turning in upon ourselves in various forms of narcissism. We need God's grace to remain free and responsible. Left to ourselves, we will soon be imprisoned.

The Trappist Father Thomas Keating provides us with a deep spiritual truth: "Interior freedom is the goal of this prayer. Not freedom to do what you like, but freedom to do what God likes—freedom to be your true self and to be transformed in Christ." This is the same thought Pope John Paul II conveyed in saying that freedom lies in obedience to God's will. This is a paradox that those who identify freedom with license cannot understand.

But Zechariah understood it as do all of us who, once imprisoned, can now speak and bless the Lord.

Meditation: What is your understanding of freedom? Note carefully the areas of your life in which you struggle to retain your God-given liberty: the physical, the psychological, and the spiritual. What do you do to foster authentic freedom?

Prayer: Lord Jesus, you came to set us free from sin and death. Open our minds and our hearts so that we might understand the beauty and the complexity of our gift of freedom. May all of our choices be in accord with your will. Only then will we know peace; only then will we live in joy.

Other Information

Readings: 2 Sam 7:1-5, 8b-12, 14a, 16; Luke 1:67-79

Scripture:
In the tender compassion of our God
    the dawn from on high shall break upon us,
      to shine on those who dwell in darkness and the shadow
        of death,
      and to guide our feet into the way of peace. (Luke 1:78-79)

Reflection: Darkness and death surround us. Our morning newspaper informs us in one section when the sun will set. In another, the obituaries, we find the listings of those who have died. Darkness and death are pushed in our face.

Our faith carries other information. Light and life will win the day because Jesus, our radiant dawn, the sun of justice, the splendor of eternal light, shines on us who are lost in the shadow of death. This belief is captured in the "O Antiphon" that has been sung, like Zechariah's canticle, for hundreds and hundreds of years: "O Radiant Dawn, splendor of eternal light, sun of justice: come, shine on those who dwell in darkness and the shadow of death."

Herein lies the battle, the struggle, the holy warfare in every mind and heart. From one quarter we are given bountiful evidence that people do live in darkness. We need but walk the corridors of our mental hospitals, observe the

confusion resulting from relativism, ponder the meaningless-
ness of much of our television entertainment, or witness the
sorrows and grief borne by divided families. Evidence also
abounds regarding the shadow of death that hovers over
traffic accidents, our hospice units, or in countries torn by
civil strife.

Our faith will be challenged. But because we trust in God's
word and the work of Jesus, we know that the sun will rise
in radiant beauty and the light of grace will illumine our
minds and hearts. By trusting in the mystery of the Resurrection, we live with the conviction that death has lost its
terrible sting. Through the paschal mystery, Jesus has freed
us from sin and death. That is why, with Zechariah and all
the prophets, we can cry out "Alleluia!"

Meditation: Take ten minutes to quietly reflect on the "O
Antiphon" quoted above. How have you experienced Jesus
as light and justice? How can you become a better agent of
God's grace?

Prayer: Jesus, our radiant dawn, shine upon us and fill us
with hope. Our days are dark and our nights are long. Death
surrounds us with its threatening fears. May your Spirit of
wisdom give us eyes of faith that see in you the extravagant
love of the Father.

CHRISTMAS AND DAYS
WITHIN ITS OCTAVE

December 25: The Nativity of the Lord (Christmas)

Vigil Mass: A Call to Vigilance

Readings: Isa 62:1-5; Acts 13:16-17, 22-25; Matt 1:1-25

Scripture:
Behold, the virgin shall conceive and bear a son,
  and they shall name him Emmanuel,
which means "God is with us." (Matt 1:23)

Reflection: In the opening prayer for this Vigil Mass we pray: "God of endless ages, Father of all goodness, we keep vigil for the dawn of salvation and the birth of your Son." We keep vigil! We are people called to be alert and watchful for the manifestation of a God who is always with us.

In celebrating Christmas, we are given a unique revelation of God in Jesus. Jesus is the Word made flesh, coming into history in a particular place and at a particular time.

But it is all too easy to be non-vigilant! We become numb by eating and drinking too much, by getting caught up in entertainment or pleasure, by pursuing wealth and power as if they were the source of happiness. Insensitivity to things divine means that we will miss the meaning of life. Vigilance is a way of life, costly and demanding. But then, it is the only true and authentic way to live a Christian life.

Our challenge is to be vigilant not only at Christmas time or during the season of Advent or Lent. Rather, we are to be watchful as the Lord appears to us through the course of our ordinary lives. If we are awake, we will notice Jesus in the cry of the poor, in the stranger who has no home, in the counsel of a teacher, in the love of a grandmother, and, yes, in the times of suffering and trial. Jesus' presence is ubiquitous; Jesus is everywhere revealing the love and forgiveness of the Father.

On this Vigil Night we sing special songs: "Joy to the World," "Silent Night," and "O Come All Ye Faithful." How can we not sing when the Lord is near in such a special celebration? Though the world is in darkness we sense that the dawn is near. There is more than a light at the end of the tunnel. Jesus himself, the light of the world, will scatter the darkness of sin and death. He will set us free.

Meditation: How observant are you? Make a list of things you have noticed during the past week. Do they show a high or low level of vigilance?

Prayer: Loving God, you call us to be a vigilant people, always on the watch for your coming. We are grateful you sent your Son to take on our humanity. Grant us the grace to be alert to the moment of grace and responsive to whatever you ask of us. May we not sleepwalk through life.

Mass at Midnight: Jesus, the Prince of Peace

Readings: Isa 9:1-6; Titus 2:11-14; Luke 2:1-14

Scripture:
For a child is born to us, a son is given us;
    upon his shoulder dominion rests.
They name him Wonder-Counselor, God-Hero,
    Father-Forever, Prince of Peace. (Isa 9:5)

Reflection: Jesus is the Prince of Peace. He came among us to restore our relationship with the Father, to bring us liberty, and to free us from the fear of death and the consequences of sin. In other words, his mission was one of peace.

The gospel for this Midnight Mass tells of the angels calming the shepherds: "Do not be afraid; for behold, I proclaim to you good news of great joy that will be for all the people" (Luke 2:10). Whenever we experience the unknown or hear whispers of the unexpected, the human heart becomes afraid. Be it a winter storm or the news of an illness or the rumors of war, we can feel our peace slipping away. What was ordered and right is now chaotic and wrong. We are afraid and anxiety can overwhelm our lives.

Jesus came into our human situation. He came to restore our relationships with the Father and with each other. As the Prince of Peace, Jesus calls us to truth and charity, to freedom and justice. Only when we become agents of these four qualities will peace reign in our hearts and in our world.

For many families, Christmas is a time of peace. Families that have been scattered gather together for meals and worship, for celebration and the exchange of gifts. But for other families and some single individuals, Christmas is a difficult time. Though Jesus comes to establish peace, many experience broken relationships, deep loneliness, or for some, even despair. For these individuals watching the joy of integral families and relationships, Christmas is an extraordinarily difficult time.

We need God's blessing here, for all of us. At the end of the liturgy at this Midnight Mass we pray: "When the Word became man, earth was joined to heaven. May he give you his peace and good will, and fellowship with all the heavenly host." And to this reverent request, we cry out: Amen!

Meditation: In what ways can you become an agent of peace during this Christmas season? Reflect on those individuals who have brought you truth, shared their love, been agents of freedom and justice. Thank them at the earliest opportunity.

Prayer: Jesus, Prince of Peace and Lord of life, we long to be in right relationships with you, with our fellow pilgrims, indeed, with ourselves. Heal us and allows us to experience the peace of your Father, which is beyond all understanding.

Mass at Dawn: The Caverns of the Heart

Readings: Isa 62:11-12; Titus 3:4-7; Luke 2:15-20

Scripture:
And Mary kept all these things,
  reflecting on them in her heart. (Luke 2:19)

Reflection: Certain educational theories emphasize the power of rote memory. By putting a poem or song or insightful quotation in your heart and in your mind, one develops a rich treasury from which these nourishing tidbits can be called forth at will. If we don't intentionally fill our hearts with truth and beauty, other things will enter to occupy the space, much to our detriment—or sanity if it's some inane song that gets stuck in our head.

Mary stored certain events in her heart and reflected upon them as she saw fit. What events and things? How the angel Gabriel came to her, how she and Elizabeth spent three months together sharing their joys and concerns, how the shepherds came to confirm the way God's plan of salvation was being worked out. Mary's heart was filled with thoughts and feelings that dealt with God's mysterious activities in her life.

Saint Paul's heart was also a treasury of grace. Paul had experienced God's love and kindness through rebirth in Jesus and the renewal of the Holy Spirit. Paul pondered the grace of justification and the hope of eternal life. And all of this, not because he was deserving, but because of the mercy of God. Paul's heart was bursting with gratitude and joy. His letters enable us to roam through the vast caverns of his mind and heart.

And Isaiah the prophet? What about his heart? It contained the good news of the savior's coming. As a prophet he had a message about how the people would become holy and redeemed through God's gracious will. His mission was to fill the hearts of his people with hope. They are not forsaken or abandoned; God is always with them.

The Carmelite poet Jessica Powers wrote: ". . . for what is heard in the heart, there is no speech at all." Surely, no words or language can capture the mysterious life of what happens in our heart. And yet, we do find some words that attempt to express the affectivity we feel when God has done great things for us. Mary's "Magnificat," her great song of praise, came right from the heart and has been sung by the church ever since.

Meditation: What are the things that you have stored in your heart? Ponder the Scriptures and find three or four passages that are well worth memorizing. Perhaps Galatians 6:2, Revelation 3:20, or Isaiah 43:1-4.

Prayer: God of truth and love, fill our hearts with your wisdom. You have done great things for all of us, and these events deserve to be stored in our hearts. Grace us with the language to share your grace with others. May we never take any of your gifts for granted.

Mass during the Day: God's Smile

Readings: Isa 52:7-10; Heb 1:1-6; John 1:1-18

Scripture:
And the Word became flesh
and made his dwelling among us,
and we saw his glory,
the glory as of the Father's only Son,
full of grace and truth. (John 1:14)

Reflection: In his classic poem "Tyger, Tyger," William Blake asks one of those foundational questions of life. After describing the fierceness of the tiger, the poet inquires whether or not God smiled "at his work to see." Was it possible for the God who made the gentle lamb also to make the terrifying tiger? Of course, we know that the answer is yes.

God's smile! A smile is a type of incarnation wherein the affection and joy in our hearts take on visibility. A smile crosses the face and we know we are dwelling near an affirming presence.

Jesus is God's smile. Jesus is the Word made flesh, giving visibility to the fullness of God's truth and love. Jesus, born of Mary, was from the beginning, and all things were made through him. God's smile has continued through the ages as God delights in his people. Despite sin and darkness, God has remained faithful, and the mystery of the Incarnation continues to be the bedrock of our faith.

One can almost see the smile on the prophet Isaiah's face as he describes the glad tidings and good news of the Lord's restoration of Zion. Isaiah urges the people to break out into song, for God has comforted his people. God's salvation calls for shouts of joy. No longer can the people be dour, for redemption is at hand. For us, the good news and glad tidings are revealed in the Word made flesh, our Lord Jesus Christ.

The author of the book of Hebrews gives us cause for smiling. God has spoken anew in Jesus and the partial messages of the past are superseded. Here is news that not only causes us to smile but also invites us to kneel in solemn worship. The Son of God is among us. Our Creator has given us a Redeemer. When God smiles on us through Jesus in the Incarnation, we know we are cared for and loved.

Meditation: In what sense is Jesus the smile of God? Reflect on the meaning of a smile both in its being received and in its giving.

Prayer: Word made flesh, deepen our love for you. You have come among us for our salvation. You continue to dwell among us through the sacraments. May we daily experience your smile and then, having experienced your love, share it with others.

December 26: Feast of St. Stephen, First Martyr (optional)

Life and Death: Side by Side

Readings: Acts 6:8-10; 7:54-59; Matt 10:17-22

Scripture:
Into your hands I commend my spirit;
   you will redeem me, O LORD, O faithful God.
I will rejoice and be glad because of your mercy. (Ps 31:6, 8a)

Reflection: The Christmas mystery focuses on life, the birth of our Messiah. But immediately after we celebrate this great and joyful mystery, the liturgical calendar turns our eyes to the mystery of death as we read about St. Stephen's martyrdom. Life and death! With great realism we are asked to ponder the whole of the Christian life.

Jesus warned his disciples about the cost of discipleship: rejection, scourging, and death. Even in the sacred bonds of families there will be betrayal. Yet in all this we are called to trust in God and in the power of the Holy Spirit that is always at hand. We are not left alone; we are accompanied every step of the journey.

Saint Stephen lived this trust. He commended his spirit to the Lord just as Jesus commended his Spirit to his Father. Stephen's "Lord Jesus, receive my spirit" manifests the depth of his faith. This courageous utterance also shows the power of the Holy Spirit working in the heart of a man who is being stoned to death. Amazing courage! Amazing faith! Amazing grace!

We do well to note that as Stephen was being stoned to death, a young man named Saul stood by as cloaks were placed at his feet. Although Saul's conversion was down the road a pace, perhaps this experience of a person being killed for his faith worked something in the heart of Saul that readied him to say yes to Jesus on that road to Damascus. Whatever the case, Saul became Paul and embraced the same martyrdom as Stephen. He gave his life for the cause of the Gospel.

Death does follow birth. But both Stephen and Paul, because of their faith in the resurrected Lord, knew the good news that life followed death. Because they believed in Jesus and were faithful to his word, they were given the gift of eternal life.

Meditation: Do you find it strange that the church celebrates martyrdom a day after the birth of the Lord? Memorize the refrain, "Into your hands, O Lord, I commend my spirit" and use it as a night prayer. What do you think went on in the heart of Saul?

Prayer: Saint Stephen, pray for us. Pray that like you, we too may have the gift of faith and courage in following Jesus. Assist us on our journey so that we may never lose sight of Jesus dwelling with the Father and interceding for us. May we too rejoice and be glad because of God's mercy.

December 27: Feast of Saint John, Apostle and Evangelist

Complete Joy

Readings: 1 John 1:1-4; John 20:1a, 2-8

Scripture:
We are writing this so that our joy may be complete.
   (1 John 1:4)

Reflection: Both Beethoven and Schubert were composers of "unfinished symphonies." Yet Schubert's 8th has been called one of the near "perfectly complete" symphonies as we know it today. John the Evangelist started a life of joyful discipleship by following Jesus. Yet he realized that he had to tell others of this new way of life if his joy was to be complete. Not to have done so would have left the world with yet another unfinished song, an incomplete joy.

John writes with some specificity. In communicating his experience of Jesus, John claims that he has seen, heard, and touched the very Word of life, Jesus the Lord. John walked with the Son of God. That grace of fellowship was not solely for this apostle. Rather, what was received—this friendship with God in Jesus—was to be offered to everyone John met. Unless this was done by word or deed, John's great joy would not have reached completion, fullness of being.

In today's gospel we sense not just the lack of joy but deep sadness. Jesus had been crucified, taken down from the cross, and buried. Now, the tomb was empty—sorrow upon sorrow.

We can crawl into the hearts of Mary Magdalene, Simon Peter, and the beloved disciple, and feel the panic and fear that they were feeling. But the gospel ends with great cause for joy: "Then the other disciple also went in, the one who had arrived at the tomb first, and he saw and believed" (John 20:8). Belief is the parent of joy.

Saint John experienced what many of us do: we cannot fall in love, see a magnificent piece of art, discover a great poem, hear a beautiful piece of music, and keep silent. Something compels us to share those experiences lest they remain incomplete. We must bring to term God's grace if we are to live genuine, mature, and joyful lives. So we listen to Wordsworth: "'It is an injury,' said I, 'to this day / To think of any thing but present joy.'"

In sharing our present joys, we recall that both Schubert's 8th and the words of John the evangelist, though incomplete, fill us with a sense of longing for the perfect—the joy that will be complete only at the end of our earthly life.

Meditation: Are you good at bringing to term the projects you are given to do? Reflect on all the times that you experienced joy. What were the ingredients of that grace? Did grace come from sharing your joy with someone?

Prayer: God of love, joy, and peace, give us the grace to complete the good work you have begun in us. Let our lives be complete and full. Through the gift of the Holy Spirit may our lives be a completed symphony. May others experience joy in our sharing with them the great things you have done for us.

DECEMBER 28–JANUARY 3

December 28:
Feast of the Holy Family of Jesus, Mary, and Joseph
(Catholic Church)

The Fourth Day in the Octave of Christmas
(Episcopal Church)

The Call to Community

Readings: Sir 3:2-6, 12-14; Col 3:12-21; Luke 2:22-40

Scripture:
The child's father and mother were amazed at what was
said about him. (Luke 2:33)

Reflection: Family life is a source of great joy and great anxiety. When relationships are running smoothly, where the
qualities mentioned by St. Paul—heartfelt compassion, kindness, humility, gentleness, and forgiveness—are present, then
there is peace. But when things are awry—lack of honor and
respect, a want of obedience and reverence—then great
suffering sweeps through the house and beyond.

We know that Jesus was destined for the rise and fall of
many. Because of this, we sense that trouble lies ahead. Jesus'
presentation in the temple was a moment of great joy. Twelve
years after the presentation, Mary and Joseph experienced
"great anxiety" when they did not know where Jesus was.
A missing child! Those words strike terror in the heart of
every parent. No words can capture the depth of fear that
such a situation inflicts on the soul. Fortunately for Mary and

Joseph, Jesus was found and the anxiety disappeared. The family was once again intact. Peace reigned as they headed back home and plunged into the hidden life of the Lord.

On this Feast of the Holy Family we do well to reflect upon the values that express God's will. The Scriptures are clear: community is at the heart of our Christian existence. In the Trinity, we see a community of persons—Father, Son, and Spirit. It is from this Triune source that the divine works of creation, redemption, and sanctification originate. Because we are made in the image and likeness of this God, we are called to union with God and with others.

Family is about striving for oneness. But the web of relationships between husband and wife, among parents and children and extended family, mean that only through disciplined effort and much sacrifice will that goal be accomplished. But, with God's help, it can be and often is.

Meditation: Reflect on your family of origin. Offer a prayer of gratitude for all the blessings that came your way; offer a prayer for healing where the wounds are still raw. What can you do today to strengthen family bonds?

Prayer: Triune God, help us understand the call to community. Self-preoccupation is so strong; individualism in our culture runs rampant. Grace us with your sacrificial love so that we might further your plan of union and unity. Unless you are with us, we cannot succeed. With you, everything is possible.

December 29: The Fifth Day in the Octave of Christmas
St. Thomas Becket, Bishop and Martyr (optional)

A Life Well Lived

Readings: 1 John 2:3-11; Luke 2:22-35

Scripture:
Now there was a man in Jerusalem whose name was Simeon.
This man was righteous and devout,
  awaiting the consolation of Israel,
  and the Holy Spirit was upon him. (Luke 2:25)

Reflection: Cicero, the great Roman orator and statesman, wrote a discourse on old age, *De Senectute*. Cicero's advice was essentially this: if prior to old age one pursues useful knowledge, practices virtues, and performs deeds that are honorable, then this "well-spent life" will serve one well in one's later years.

Simeon lived a good life. In old age he awaited God's promise of a messiah. His well-spent life consisted of righteousness and sincere devotion. Simeon knew he was under the influence of the Holy Spirit. It was God's grace that enabled him to be devout and righteous and filled with faith. Simeon kept God's commandment and lived in the light.

Saint Thomas Becket (1118–1170) did not have to contend with old age. He was the Archbishop of Canterbury and stood up to King Henry II when the king attempted to exert his political power over the church. In this historical event, we witness the perpetual struggle between light and dark. Though the darkness seemed to triumph when Becket was murdered in the cathedral, we know that in the end the blood of this martyr brought much light and faith in England.

As archbishop, Thomas Becket daily joined Simeon in praying that great nighttime prayer, the *Nunc Dimittis*: "Lord, now let your servant go in peace; / your word has been fulfilled: / my own eyes have seen the salvation / which you prepared in the sight of every people, / a light to reveal you to the nations / and the glory of your people Israel" (Luke 2:29-32).

We are all aging. If our life is well spent by living in the light and keeping God's commandments, we will have nothing to fear in our golden years.

Meditation: What is the best way to prepare for old age? Reflect upon one or two people you know who have grown old gracefully. How did they live their lives? What qualities did they have? What qualities would you like to develop?

Prayer: God of the old and young, help all of us to live in your light and to embrace your call, whatever it may be. As the years fly by, we long to live in your presence and to respond to your slightest stirrings. We will die as we live; we hope that will be in your loving presence.

December 30: The Sixth Day in the Octave of Christmas

Fasting, Prayer, and Service

Readings: 1 John 2:12-17; Luke 2:36-40

Scripture:
There was a prophetess, Anna. . . .
She never left the temple,
    but worshiped night and day with fasting and prayer.
        (Luke 2:36-37)

Reflection: Anna, the prophetess, did three things in her spiritual life. She fasted, she prayed, and she served. What she did, every Christian is asked to do.

Fasting. Each of us has a relationship with ourselves and that relationship is to be kept ordered and whole. By means of mortification and asceticism we deny ourselves of those things that block the fullness of life. Fasting is pointed toward life; asceticism channels energies toward full growth. Fasting creates an empty space that makes room for the Lord. No longer will addictions and dissipation govern our day. Anna knew the value and the necessity of asceticism—it was necessary if she was to be free for the Lord.

Prayer. To pray is to enter into a mysterious dialogue between God and self. Both God and the individual (and the community in public worship) are listeners and speakers. God always takes the initiative and we, at first, are responders. Prayer protects and promotes a second relationship in our spiritual life: our relationship with a Triune God. Through serious conversation and honest communication with God, we come to discern God's will and respond to what the Lord is asking of us. Anna prayed day and night; her relationship with God was one of intimacy.

Service. As a prophetess, Anna served the community. Her vocation was one of evangelization. She spoke about the child Jesus to anyone awaiting the message of salvation. Here she was, at age eighty-four, still fulfilling her vocation. Service deals with the third relationship of spirituality: our relationship with our sisters and brothers. The need that Anna met was one of truth; her God-given gift was one of prophecy.

As we approach a new year, we might do well to examine the quality of our own asceticism, prayer, and service. May we emulate Anna in each of these categories.

Meditation: Of the three components of spirituality—fasting, prayer, and service—which is strongest in your life and which is the weakest? What is God asking of you in terms of spiritual growth? What is your response? What would you like your response to be?

Prayer: Gracious God, you gifted Anna with a full life. She responded to your will and was given the great revelation of Jesus. Open our minds and hearts to the gift of your Son. Send your Spirit to help us understand our own giftedness and the needs we are to address as faithful and obedient servants of you, our God. We ask this through the same Christ, our Lord.

Truth

Readings: 1 John 2:18-21; John 1:1-18

Scripture:
I write to you not because you do not know the truth
but because you do, and because every lie is alien to the
truth. (1 John 2:21)

Reflection: Scholars have devoted their lives to the field of epistemology, the study of how we know and how we strive to discover the truth. Saint John was an epistemologist in that he was deeply concerned with knowledge and how the truth, once gained, can set us free. The truth that he communicated was that God's love was revealed in Jesus and that Jesus is the Christ, the anointed Messiah and savior of humankind.

The first chapter of John's gospel is filled with truth claims: that Jesus, the Word, was with God for all eternity; that the Word was God; that all things were made through him; that God became flesh in Jesus; that God's enduring love and glory came through Jesus. All of this comes to us through revelation and demands faith. On its own, our finite reason is unable to come to the knowledge of such truths.

John the Baptist testified to the light, challenging people to live in the truth. What was true in John's day is also true in ours. Not only is there a lack of knowledge about God but there are philosophies and schools of thought that claim we cannot know, that truth is impossible. Skeptics and cynics abound. Atheists too populate our land.

A caution is in order. Lest we become arrogant in our faith, we must humbly admit that our reason is finite, that our language is always inadequate in attempting to describe the mystery of God, and that doubting is part of the human condition. There are few things more obnoxious than people of faith arrogantly claiming that they have the truth all sewed up. We live in mystery, and we need to humbly admit that our knowledge is limited and needs constant growth and reformulation.

In his autobiographical piece *The Seven Storey Mountain*, Thomas Merton writes: "The beginning of love is truth, and before He will give us His love, God must cleanse our souls of the lies that are in them."

Meditation: In what sense is the beginning of love truth? Make a list of the truths that govern your spiritual life. Where do you go to find the truth?

Prayer: God of love and truth, guide our minds and hearts in your ways. Our reason is so limited; our hearts are so narrow. Send your Spirit to enlighten us to see your glory in Jesus; send your Spirit to expand our hearts to embrace the mystery of love. Come, Holy Spirit, come.

January 1: Solemnity of Mary, Mother of God
(Catholic Church)

The Holy Name
(Episcopal Church)

Fullness of Time

Readings: Num 6:22-27; Gal 4:4-7; Luke 2:16-21

Scripture:
When the fullness of time had come, God sent his Son,
   born of a woman, born under the law,
   to ransom those under the law,
   so that we might receive adoption as sons. (Gal 4:4-5)

Reflection: In his novel *The Second Coming*, Walker Percy writes of one of the characters: "For her, too, it was a question of time. What would she do with time? Was there something she was supposed to do?"

Mary, the Mother of God, knew that she was to do something with the gift of time that God gave her. Her mission was to bear Jesus, the savior of the world. Mary's time was well spent for she did God's will graciously and generously because of her love of God and others.

Saint Paul speaks of the "fullness of time." The mystery of the Incarnation meant that eternity had crossed the boundaries of time and plunged headlong into history. God's love took on flesh. Now, in time and space, the glory of God would be revealed for all who had the eyes of faith. Every bush could be seen as burning, every sunbeam containing some manifestation of the divine.

Through this fullness of time we are all offered the gift of adoption. Through Jesus a new relationship is possible between the divine and the human. We are no longer strangers and aliens. Rather, through the coming of Christ, we are invited into the family of God wherein we know the intimacy of God and the call to build the kingdom.

The shepherds were privileged to see the fullness of time in a manger; they were also privileged to go and tell it on the mountain. Their speech now caused amazement. And Mary, reflecting on this great event in her heart, praised God for the marvelous things he had done for her and the world.

Time is a gift. No matter how much time we have, we are to use it well. Saint Augustine says in one of his spiritual exercises: "I must appoint set times, set aside certain hours for the health of my soul." Mary did that and by so doing continued to stay in touch with Eternity, the mystery of God in her Son and in her gentle heart.

Meditation: What value do you assign to time? What do you ponder in your heart? Take out your personal calendar and write in times dedicated to the health of your soul.

Prayer: Eternal and Triune God, you came into history to offer us the fullness of life in the fullness of time. The eternal Now gathers all times—past, present, and future—into the embrace of your extravagant love. May we treasure every hour of every day as a gift from you. May we rejoice in our adoption as your daughters and sons.

January 2:
Memorial of Sts. Basil the Great and Gregory Nazianzen
Bishops and Doctors of the Church

Eternal Life

Readings: 1 John 2:22-28; John 1:19-28

Scripture:
And this is the promise that he made us: eternal life.
(1 John 2:25)

Reflection: We time-bound creatures find it difficult to comprehend the notion of eternity, more specifically, eternal life. Does not everything seem to come to an end? The vulnerable flowers of spring, the strong lion of the jungle, the great castles and forts of the Middle Ages, and even the pyramids of Egypt wear down and fade. Yet we are haunted by the possibility of "forever."

The notion of eternal life need not rely on mere human philosophy. We hear time and time again in the Bible that we are bound for glory. In Jesus, we are promised eternal life. This revelation is given to us lest we be deceived and think that temporality wins the day.

The two great saints whose feast we celebrate today, Saint Basil the Great and Saint Gregory Nazianzen, believed in the word of God. Like John the Baptist before them, they testified to the person of Jesus and were voices crying out in the desert. They taught about the mystery of eternal life and the fidelity of God to his promises. They presented a vision of life that told this startling news: through the mystery of the resurrection both death and sin have been overcome. God's love is eternal, it is forever.

In his classic play *Our Town*, Thornton Wilder laments through the character of the stage manager that although certain truths have been taught for thousands of years, we tend to forget or lose sight of them. He concludes by saying that in the depth of everyone there is something eternal, something that lasts forever. Saints Basil and Gregory, John the Baptist, and Jesus himself, have all taught this truth: eternal life is our destiny. We cannot afford to forget this graced piece of wisdom.

Belief in eternal life should have a major impact on our daily life and the decisions that we make. We do not "eat, drink, and be merry" as if this life of time and space is all there is. Rather, we have our eyes set on our ultimate union with God and our human community. It is this vision that influences our attitudes and behavior. It colors our days and influences our every decision.

Meditation: Do you sense "that something eternal" deep down within you? What is your attitude toward death: extinction or liberation? How does the notion of eternity affect the way that you live your daily life?

Prayer: Lord God, in Jesus you have promised us the grace of eternal life. Deepen our faith that we might embrace your word in all its fullness. May everything we say and do be done under the eye of Eternity. Come, Spirit of wisdom, come.

The Most Holy Name of Jesus

Readings: 1 John 2:29–3:6; John 1:29-34

Scripture:
John the Baptist saw Jesus coming toward him and said,
   "Behold, the Lamb of God, who takes away the sin of
      the world." (John 1:29)

Reflection: William Blake, the English poet, wrote some
verse for children. One of his poems, "Little Lamb," has the
poet (or reader) addressing the lamb in these words: "I a
child & thou a lamb, / We are called by his name."
   John the Baptist calls Jesus a lamb, the Lamb of God. The
Baptist saw far into the future. His vision was one of Jesus
giving himself for the salvation of the world by shedding
his blood. As a lamb is led to slaughter to feed many, so too
Jesus would become food for the world. All Christians are
called to participate in this sacrificial life. Today we celebrate
the Holy Name of Jesus. There are many names that describe
different aspects of his very being: Son of God, Son of Mary,
Redeemer and Savior, Brother and Friend, Master and
Teacher, and, yes, Lamb of God. By honoring the name, we
honor the person. No one name can capture the mystery, so
we use language in multiple ways to peel away different
layers of a personality.

John the Baptist saw Jesus approaching him. As a Mystical Body, we too know that Jesus continues to come into our lives. If we have the wisdom of the Baptist, we can name some of those comings: Jesus in the cry of the poor, Jesus in the exiled, Jesus in the terminally ill, Jesus in the scholar or artist or engineer.

But always, Eucharist after Eucharist, we come back to finding Jesus in the symbol of a lamb. It is precisely in the giving of Jesus' life for the salvation of the world that we come to know that we are loved and forgiven.

In the First Letter of John we read: "See what love the Father has bestowed on us that we may be called the children of God" (3:1a). This is made possible by the obedience of Jesus who came and took our sins on himself. Jesus became the slain lamb risen to new life. When we say the name of Jesus, we profess our belief in the mystery of the Incarnation and of his dying and rising.

Meditation: When you sing the "Lamb of God" at Mass, what do you feel in your heart? What are your favorite names for Jesus? How has your understanding of Jesus changed over the years? Has that changed your favorite names for Jesus?

Prayer: Jesus, you are the Lamb of God, the one who takes away the sins of the world and who has conquered death. May we grow in knowledge of you and learn to find a language to help us express our faith in you to others. May we honor your name always.

EPIPHANY AND
BAPTISM OF THE LORD

Stewards of Grace

Readings: Isa 60:1-6; Eph 3:2-3a, 5-6; Matt 2:1-12

Scripture:
You have heard of the stewardship of God's grace
  that was given to me for your benefit,
    namely, that the mystery was made known to me by
      revelation. (Eph 3:2-3a)

Reflection: Each of us is called to a life of stewardship. God has given to everyone a special gift that is to be nurtured and shared with others. What that grace is depends upon God's providence. Whether that gift and grace is received, developed, and shared depends upon the exercise of human freedom, our willingness to cooperate with the grace of God.

Isaiah was a good steward and his gift was the prophetic one of both calling people to conversion and giving them a deep sense of hope. In the passage for today, Isaiah is eloquent in describing the glory and radiance of God's coming. For those who have faith, hearts will throb and overflow with joy and God will be praised and blessed for such divine goodness. Isaiah was gifted with a unique revelation that invited people into the mystery of God's love and goodness.

Saint Paul was graced with the mystery of Jesus. In a unique revelation, Paul came to see that in Jesus all people have access to salvation. More, we are all members of a single body and God is Father of all. This insight is revolutionary and has the power, if embraced and lived, to alter human history in a radical way. Although St. Paul exercised his vocation as a steward, many people did not accept his preaching.

And the stewardship given to the magi? Deliver gifts to a newborn babe beneath a distant star! Their primary gift was, not gold, frankincense, or myrrh, but the homage of faith. They came to adore; they came to see a child who would be king. Here is a gift that all of us can bring on this feast of Epiphany—our adoration and worship of our savior, Jesus, the Christ, the King of Kings.

The preface for today's Mass describes the mystery that St. Paul proclaimed, that Isaiah experienced, that the magi saw: "Today you revealed in Christ your eternal plan of salvation and showed him as the light of all peoples."

Meditation: What stewardship role has God assigned to you? What gift and knowledge are you called to share with others? Pause and thank those who have been stewards to you on your journey of faith.

Prayer: Jesus, light of all nations, you who came to scatter the darkness of sin and death. May we embrace your light and share it with others. May we embrace your love and pass it on to all we meet. Come, Lord Jesus, come into our fragile and broken world.

January 5: Memorial of St. John Neumann, Bishop

The Call to Discernment

Readings: 1 John 3:22–4:6; Matt 4:12-17, 23-25

Scripture:
Beloved, do not trust every spirit
  but test the spirits to see whether they belong to God,
  because many false prophets have gone out into the world.
    (1 John 4:1)

Reflection: Saint John Neumann (1811–1860) was born in Bohemia. Throughout his life Neumann had to discern what God was calling him to do. Neumann's canonization in 1977 affirmed that his discernment was of God. Neumann discerned that God called him to the priesthood, that he was called to leave his native land and come to the American missions, that as bishop of Philadelphia he was to work with immigrants and to build parish schools. Surely much prayer went into making these decisions, which enriched the church in so many different ways.

Jesus was also in the business of reflecting on and carrying out his Father's will. Filled with the Spirit, Jesus taught, healed, and proclaimed the good news of God's love and mercy. He discerned that the Father's kingdom was near and that everyone must reform and turn from darkness to the light. His discernment took him into the lives of those racked with pain, possessed by demons, and those who were mentally unstable.

Graced discernment means that we are doing what is pleasing in God's sight. In the First Letter of John we know that this involves keeping the commandments. By so doing we remain in Christ and Christ in us. Always we must be on alert since deception is forever competing with the truth. To sort all this out we need the gift of the Holy Spirit.

Father Jon Sobrino got it right: "The disciple living today . . . does possess one ultimate criterion for correct discernment, that is, Jesus himself." As disciples we are to place all of our attitudes, behaviors, and inspirations up against the Gospel. If there is harmony between what we are doing and the life of Jesus, we are on the right track. Surely, this was true in St. John Neumann's decisions to work with immigrants and in the education of children.

Meditation: What has been your experience of discerning truth from falsity? Before making decisions, do you invoke the Spirit for the gift of discernment? Name one experience of discernment that went well and one that went poorly. What caused the discernment to have these results?

Prayer: Come, Holy Spirit, and grant us the gift of wisdom and discernment. Life gets very complex and we find it difficult to decide rightly. Help us to see what is truly pleasing to you, then to name that activity, and finally to do it.

January 6
(Catholic Church)

The Epiphany
(Episcopal Church; see above, January 4)

Love: A Path to Knowledge

Readings: 1 John 4:7-10; Mark 6:34-44

Scripture:
Beloved, let us love one another,
    because love is of God;
    everyone who loves is begotten by God and knows God.
        (1 John 4:7)

Reflection: The question of "how do we know" is a perennial one and it was asked from the very start of recorded philosophy. The same is true about love: what is it? How do we know that we are loving? What are its qualities?

In the First Letter of John we are given an insight into the knowledge/love questions. We are told that love is a path to knowledge. Since love is of God and the lover participates in love, then the lover gains in his or her knowledge of who God is. This is somewhat of a reversal in that many philosophers hold that you cannot love what you do not know. In other words, knowledge comes first and then love becomes a possibility.

But here we find a different approach. If you want to know about God, first be a loving person. The rationale for this position is this: God is love. We participate in God's life by loving as God loved.

Mother Teresa of Calcutta was not a great theologian. Yet, her knowledge of God was profound. In her service to the poorest of the poor, she experienced the presence of Christ in ways that no classroom or textbook could convey. Her knowledge was experiential and genuine. It flowed from a loving heart and instilled in her a humble wisdom. She told the world that we had to bring the beauty of God's love to all we meet.

All kinds of discussions go on concerning the existence and nature of God. Huge tomes are written on God's qualities. Questions are raised about the essence of the Trinity and various understandings of the Incarnation, the two central doctrines of Christianity. All of this is both necessary and interesting. But then there is the simple, humble, loving person who silently progresses in an authentic knowledge of God just by showing respect, active concern, and reverence for others.

Meditation: How much do you know about God? Where did this knowledge come from? Spend some time today loving someone in need. How does that deed affect your theology?

Prayer: Lord, you have given the gifts of knowledge and love. Through these graces we become more and more like you. Our thirst for knowledge is unending; your hunger to love and be loved is insatiable. Send your Spirit of love and knowledge into our hearts that we might further your kingdom and come to an intimate knowledge of your life.

Love versus Fear

Readings: 1 John 4:11-18; Mark 6:45-52

Scripture:
There is no fear in love,
but perfect love drives out fear. (1 John 4:18a)

Reflection: No one can adequately describe the fear and
panic of the passengers on the planes that were hijacked on
9/11. Even those steeped in love must have shuddered
violently when they realized that they were destined to die.
Love is powerful, but so is fear.

The disciples of Jesus were frightened by the threat to their
lives in the middle of the night as the waves and wind
mounted in intensity. Their demise seemed imminent.
Though they had love in their hearts, their bodies and spirits
were deeply frightened and Jesus had to come and alleviate
their fear. But even in his coming they were frightened as he
walked toward them on the waves. Indeed, the disciples
were taken aback by these happenings as they witnessed the
power of God in creation and in their hearts.

Various phrases that express aspects of our culture become
popular. Pope John Paul II talked often about "the culture
of death," referring to abortion, war, and other human activities that threaten the dignity of the human person. Others
have talked about "the culture of disbelief" or "the culture

of complaint." But there seems to be a perennial phenomenon: "the culture of fear"! So much energy is directed to all those things that threaten our safety, sometimes to such an extent that we are paralyzed.

So, what is an alternative? Again, Pope John Paul II has spoken eloquently of "a civilization of love." It is love of God and neighbor, it is love of self and creation that empower us to believe that in the end all will be well. God is love, and that grace drives out those false fears that paralyze mind, body, and spirit.

One of the great saints of the church, Catherine of Siena, reiterated the insight from St. John's letter when she wrote: "For the soul is always afraid until she has attained true love." In some mysterious way, the disciples of Jesus experienced the extravagant love and mercy of God in Jesus and were then empowered to give their lives to the Gospel to the point of martyrdom. True love does drive out all false fear from the human heart.

Meditation: What are your fears? Have you had any experiences in which your fears were conquered because of the loving presence of a parent or friend? Is there any such thing as a healthy or graced fear?

Prayer: Lord Jesus, come to us in the storms of life when we feel threatened by any sort of harm or violence. Instill in us the power of love so that we are not paralyzed by the anxieties of life. May we hear your words—"Do not be afraid"—over and over again. Open our minds to the mystery of your love.

January 8

Habit of Doing, Habit of Being

Readings: 1 John 4:19–5:4; Luke 4:14-22a

Scripture:
He came to Nazareth, where he had grown up,
    and went according to his custom
    into the synagogue on the sabbath day.
He stood up to read . . . (Luke 4:16)

Reflection: In 1979, the firm of Farrar, Straus, and Giroux published a book entitled *Letters of Flannery O'Connor: The Habit of Being*. In one of the letters, O'Connor shares her practice of sitting at a table every morning for several hours waiting for the creative muses to come. It was her "habit of being"—being present—that led to such a creative and productive life, though she died at age thirty-nine of lupus.

Jesus had his habits as well. One of them was to attend the synagogue on the Sabbath and to read and ponder the words of the Jewish tradition. This habit served him well as all good habits (virtues) serve us well too. The routine of doing the right thing in the right way fosters growth and spiritual development.

Habits are about doing and being. Through human effort we seek to realize our God-given potential. But there is something more than mere human effort. Jesus is explicit about the Spirit of God as the source and grounding of all good habits. Flannery O'Connor also knew that her writing habits were rooted in the "spirit" of creativity, which she did not so much "do" as receive and use. Again we are reminded by God's word that our spiritual lives are a mixture of faith and work, of gift and responsibility, of holy mutuality.

In the First Letter of John we can sense the power of God's Spirit alive in the writer. Truth permeates this passage as we hear about the command of loving both God and our neighbor. John tells us directly about who is and who is not truly a child of God. It's all about the habit of obedience, that is, of doing what God asks of us (love) so that we might exercise the habit of being his children.

Habits are powerful means of shaping our character and our destiny—the habit of doing, the habit of being, the habit of kindness.

Meditation: What habits of doing and being characterize your life? Make a list of your virtues and vices. What actions can you take to foster your virtues and eliminate your vices?

Prayer: Gracious God, you are a God of love and kindness. Instill in us good habits—the virtue of charity, the virtue of courage, the virtue of wisdom. Then, with you, we will be able to live life to the fullest.

January 9

Grace of Health

Readings: 1 John 5:5-13; Luke 5:12-16

Scripture:
It happened that there was a man full of leprosy in one of
the towns where Jesus was;
and when he saw Jesus,
he fell prostrate, pleaded with him, and said,
"Lord, if you wish, you can make me clean." (Luke 5:12)

Reflection: Health is a great wealth. When our bodies, emotions, and spiritual faculties are functioning well, we have energy to be creative and life-giving. However, with illness comes the fact that the focus of our lives narrows to deal with the pain, anxiety, or fear. Granted, some individuals are able to transcend sickness and be creative and of service to others, but this is rather infrequent.

"[A] man full of leprosy." Not only was his body being decimated but he was also cut off from family and community. Along with the physical suffering came the psychological pain of rejection and loneliness. This man came to Jesus and made his request to be made clean. The rest of the story is well-known.

But this is also our story. All of us need healing—to be made clean—at a variety of levels. And we can be assured that Jesus wants to heal us and grant us the fullness of life.

And what do we need healing from? Our narcissism perhaps, or our pride or lust or greed? Maybe it is the unwillingness or inability to forgive some past transgression. Or we might be dealing with the leprosy of self-contempt or the disease of megalomania. Whatever it is, Jesus says to us today: "I do will it. Be made clean."

In Shakespeare's *King Lear* we are reminded: "Infirmity doth still neglect all office / Whereto our health is bound." But grace too doth neglect all office and is available to all who come to Jesus asking to be healed. God's mercy and love are universal. God's will is that all be saved, not from bodily death that comes to us all, but from eternal death that cuts us off from the source of life. Jesus came, not for the healthy and well, but for all of those in need of healing and redemption. And the good news is, that's all of us.

Meditation: In what ways has Jesus brought health and healing into your life? How has the Lord asked you to be an agent of healing for others?

Prayer: God of mercy and compassion, look upon us who stand in need of your healing power. Restore our well-being so that we might be about your work of bringing life to others. Our faith is deep because your love is near. Come, Lord Jesus, come.

January 10

Obedience and Humility

Readings: 1 John 5:14-21; John 3:22-30

Scripture:
   ". . . the best man, who stands and listens for him,
   rejoices greatly at the bridegroom's voice.
So this joy of mine has been made complete.
He must increase; I must decrease." (John 3:29b-30)

Reflection: Playing second fiddle is irksome to some but not to John the Baptist. He understood his vocation to be one of preparing the way for another. He was not the groom but the best man and it was precisely in fulfilling that role that he found his joy. Would that we knew our place in God's great design.

Two qualities of John the Baptist are evident in today's gospel: obedience and humility. Obedience is about hearing and responding to the will of another. John the Baptist heard the voice of the groom and pointed everyone in his direction. Again and again John witnesses to the fact that he is not the Messiah. Rather, his cousin Jesus is the anointed of the Lord and is the one who will save the world.

The second quality is humility as evidenced in the decreasing and increasing theme. As the groom enters the wedding feast the best man recedes into the background. The first violinist has arrived and is the one to carry the melody. The

Baptist knew his place and kept it. Jesus was to grow in recognition as John was to wane.

One of the by-products of obedience and humility is joy. This is the type of joy arising out of fidelity to one's basic calling. By doing God's will and by facing reality for what it is, the heart is flooded with joy in the rightness of things.

It is in the baptism of Jesus (tomorrow's feast) that we witness the change of focus. John's work has been completed as Jesus' ministry begins. The analogy of retirement does not quite fit since John has one last sacrifice to make—the giving of his life for the truth. This event shows how John's obedience and humility went all the way to the end.

Meditation: What roles do obedience and humility play in your life? In what sense are we all to "decrease" as we grow in Christian maturity?

Prayer: Lord Jesus, your cousin John the Baptist served you well. He prepared for your coming and stepped aside once you began your public ministry. Teach us the obedience and humility he lived. Help us to hear your voice and to follow your way. May we know our place in your plan of salvation. Grant us the grace to trust when our place seems to us to be a mystery.

The Baptismal Plunge

Readings: Isa 42:1-4, 6-7 or Isa 55:1-11; Acts 10:34-38 or
1 John 5:1-9; Mark 1:7-11

Scripture:
This is what he proclaimed:
  "One mightier than I is coming after me.
I am not worthy to stoop and loosen the thongs of his
  sandals." (Mark 1:7)

Reflection: As children many of us would stand on the dock
facing the cold spring lake and hesitate. The body simply
did not want to plunge into the icy water so, if we were not
pushed by a companion, eventually we would have to face
making the leap or going home without the experience of
living life more fully.

Jesus took the plunge. He entered fully into our humanity
with yet another piece of evidence of how extravagant God's
love is for us. Now we know that our God is an "insider"
God, one who knows the coldness of spring water, the joy
of wedding wine, the weariness of travel, the grace of human
friendship. Just as Jesus was baptized into our humanity in
this symbolic way, so too we are baptized into divine life,
offered a share in the very life of God.

John the Baptist was the agent of this graced moment. In
a sermon by St. Gregory of Nazianzen, John the Baptist is

described as the lamp standing before the sun, a voice meeting the very Word of God, a friend before the Bridegroom. We should not be surprised that John protested. How is it possible that a servant baptize and anoint a king? John understood his role clearly: as a forerunner he was to recede into the background so Jesus could take center stage. John's diminishment meant that his mission had been accomplished.

The whole purpose of the Christian existence is to participate in the life of Jesus. We too are to hear those glorious words that we are God's beloved creatures. The same Holy Spirit that descended upon Jesus is given to us in baptism and confirmation. The same mission of doing the Father's will is ours. The same destiny—fullness of life—is at the heart of our calling.

As we arise out of the baptismal font the words are whispered: "You matter!" We are indeed precious in God's eyes and the baptism of Jesus assures us of that fact.

Meditation: Have you taken the plunge into the fullness of the Christian life? Are prayer, asceticism, and service a part of your daily existence?

Prayer: Lord Jesus, in the waters of baptism you entered into the depths of our humanity. May we understand more fully the meaning of our own baptism: our call to maturity, holiness, service, community, and generosity. We long to participate in your mission and ministry. Renew today the grace of baptism in our souls.